F Is for Feelings

Goldie Millar and Lisa A. Berger

illustrated by Hazel Mitchell

free spirit
PUBLISHING®

Library of Congress Cataloging-in-Publication Data
Millar, Golden Melanie, 1972–
    F is for feelings / Goldie Millar and Lisa Berger; illustrated by Hazel Mitchell.
        pages cm
    Summary: "This alphabet book teaches young children about feelings and the idea that all emotions are natural and important. Colorful illustrations accompany the text. A section in the back provides tips and activities for parents, teachers, and caregivers to reinforce the book's themes and lessons" — Provided by publisher.
    ISBN 978-1-57542-475-0 (hardback)
    ISBN 1-57542-475-4 (hard cover)
    ISBN 978-1-57542-476-7 (soft cover)
1. Emotions—Juvenile literature. I. Berger, Lisa, 1967- II. Mitchell, Hazel, illustrator. III. Title.
    BF511.M55 2014
    152.4—dc23

                                                                                        2014011283
ISBN: 978-1-57542-476-7

Reading Level Grade 1; Interest Level Ages 3–8;
Fountas & Pinnell Guided Reading Level J

Edited by Alison Behnke
Cover and interior design by Michelle Lee Lagerroos

10 9 8
Printed in Hong Kong
P17200620

Free Spirit Publishing Inc.
6325 Sandburg Road, Suite 100
Minneapolis, MN 55427-3674
(612) 338-2068
help4kids@freespirit.com
freespirit.com

FSC
www.fsc.org
MIX
Paper from
responsible sources
FSC® C018769

Free Spirit offers competitive pricing.
Contact edsales@freespirit.com for pricing information on multiple quantity purchases.

To my fantastic and life-changing trio:
DM, EMM, and SMM

—Goldie

Connection, learning, and laughter . . .
thank you to TT, RZYBT, and RXYBT!

—Lisa

A Letter to Caring Adults

Hello, parents, teachers, grandparents, doctors, guardians, therapists, and all members of a child's community! Welcome. We are thrilled to join with you in sharing and learning about children's feelings.

Children show their feelings in many ways, including smiling, whining, yelling, singing, hitting, hugging, and laughing. All of these behaviors are ways for kids to express and communicate how they feel. *F Is for Feelings* will help you and the children in your life start a conversation about emotions. It will also help kids develop their feeling words so they can express themselves more effectively. When children learn from an early age to share and describe their emotions in healthy and supported ways, they are more likely to grow into adults who feel capable of handling life's challenges.

Traditionally, many people think of some emotions as positive, such as joy, excitement, and pride. Other feelings, such as sadness, fear, and anger, are often thought of as negative. We invite you, as a caring adult, to view all feelings as okay. Some feelings are comfortable. Others are more difficult to experience, and can be uncomfortable. You can help children understand that all emotions, comfortable or not, give us ways to understand ourselves and the world around us.

F Is for Feelings is meant to be read aloud and discussed. It gives you a place to connect and explore together with kids. We want children to ask lots of questions and to expand the conversation with drawing and dramatic play. On pages 32–35, you'll find more ideas for sharing this book with children. When you get to the end of our feelings alphabet, things are really just beginning. We hope you will enjoy the *F Is for Feelings* journey again and again!

—Goldie and Lisa

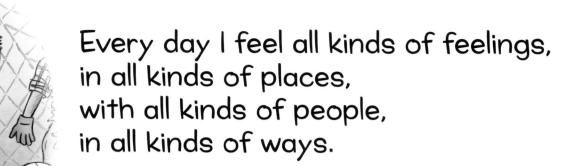

Every day I feel all kinds of feelings,
in all kinds of places,
with all kinds of people,
in all kinds of ways.

At times I feel good and other times not-so-good.

A is for afraid.

I am scared.

B is for **brave.**

Bb

I am going to be strong,
even though I feel frightened.

D is for **determined.**

I'm trying hard. I think I can do it.

E is for embarrassed.

I didn't mean to do that. I don't want anyone to laugh at me.

F is for frustrated.

I can't make it work!

G is for grumpy.

Gg

I feel grouchy about everything.
Nothing seems quite right.

10

H is for **happy.**

Hh

I am jumping for joy. I feel so glad!

I is for impatient.

Ii

I don't feel like waiting.
I want to do it NOW!

12

K is for **kind.**

I will help you. I want to do something nice.

L is for lonely.

L l

I am on my own
and I'm feeling left out.

M is for mad.

Mm

I don't like that. I'm angry!

N is for nervous.

Nn

I am not sure about this.

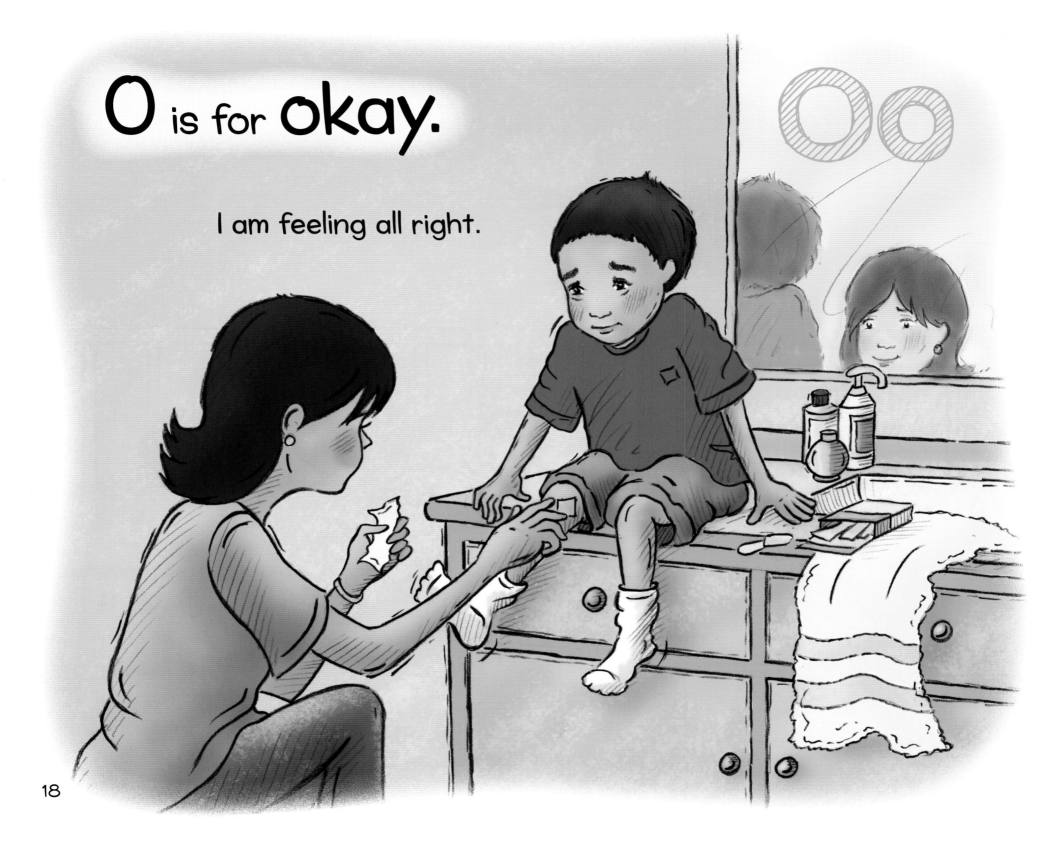

P is for proud.

Pp

I did it! I feel good about myself.

Q is for **quiet.**

I need some time all by myself. Shhh . . .

R is for **respectful.**

I care about you, and I want to show it.

S is for sad.

Ss

I feel unhappy. I'm having a hard time.

T is for **terrific.**

I feel great. I am having so much fun!

U is for **upset.**

I don't like this. This is *not* how I want things to go!

V is for **valued.**

V v

I'm glad you're listening.
I know you care.

25

W is for worried.

I don't know what will happen.

X is for excited.

I can hardly wait!

Y is for **yelling.**

Yy

I'm full of energy, and I feel like being loud!

Each day, *everyone* feels all kinds of feelings, in all kinds of places, with all kinds of people, in all kinds of ways.

30

How are YOU feeling right now?

Talking and Learning About Feelings: A Guide for Parents, Teachers, and Caregivers

Whether you are a parent, grandparent, teacher, health professional, caregiver, or other person in a child's life, you play an important role in helping children learn to identify, express, and regulate their emotions. The ability to manage emotions is linked to stronger, healthier relationships, as well as better performance in school. Knowing how to express feelings clearly is an important first step in a child's emotional development.

F Is for Feelings provides a starting point for conversations with young children about their emotions. The suggestions in this guide offer a range of ways to keep that conversation going. Some of these suggestions may be best suited for use in a classroom or with a group. Others might be better for times when you're talking with a child one-on-one. As you read and explore this book, you'll probably come up with ideas of your own. Choose, adapt, and have fun with the ones that work for you!

Read and Discuss the Book

Read the book together. Choose a picture to talk about in more detail. Ask questions about the picture and the feeling it shows. You could try these questions as a starting point:

- What do you think is happening in this picture?
- How do you think this child feels? What tells you he or she is feeling that way?
- Do you think you would feel the same as this child if you were in the same situation? Why or why not? What else might you be feeling?
- What do you think might happen next?

- Can you tell me a time when you felt the way this child does? Can you remember a time when a friend felt that way? What did you do?
- Are there pictures in the book that show how you are feeling right now? Which ones?

Follow Up with Creative Games, Songs, and Role Plays

Invite children to use their creativity as a way to explore and investigate different feelings. You can choose which suggestions to use based on the ages and interests of the child or group you're working with. Children could:

- Draw a picture of one or two of the feeling words in the book.
- Write a story using some of the book's feeling words.
- Act or physically show what one or two of the feeling words would look like (for instance, one feeling that is comfortable and one that is harder to express).
- Create a song or rhyme about one of the feelings.

- Make up a puppet show or skit telling a story about one of the feelings in the book.
- Put together their own books or collages using images from magazines to show some of the feeling words in the book.

Encourage children to share their creations. Talk about the feeling or feelings they've chosen to depict. Why did they choose that feeling? Why did they express it in the way they did?

Focus on Feelings Every Day

Children learn new skills through repetition. When you can, give them plenty of chances to practice using feeling words every day and in a variety of situations.

- Choose a feeling "word of the day" from the book and display it in a common space (such as a classroom's main board or on the family refrigerator). Each day, spend a few minutes talking about the word. Define it if needed, and discuss a few examples of times when someone might experience this feeling. Ask children about when they have felt this emotion. To build understanding further, invite children to draw faces showing expressions associated with the emotion.
- Another way to practice feeling words is to ask children at the beginning of each day to choose a word in the book that describes (or comes close to describing) how they are feeling at the moment. Thank the child for sharing and acknowledge the feeling expressed. This activity builds emotional vocabulary, and at the same time helps prepare children for learning and engaging with the day.
- Create a feelings bulletin board that displays all of the feeling words in the book, along with pictures, illustrations, and other visual representations of the different emotions.

Build a Feeling Vocabulary

F Is for Feelings introduces lots of feeling words, but there are many more. You can help children expand their emotional vocabulary by brainstorming related words and ideas.

- Ask children to come up with their own definitions of each feeling word. Encourage them to be specific and descriptive.
- Ask children to come up with similar feeling words and opposite feeling words to those in the book. For example, if you decide to talk about "H is for happy," get the brainstorming started by pointing out that a similar word to happy might be *joyful*, while an opposite word could be *sad*.
- Invite the child or the group to come up with other feeling words that begin with each letter of the alphabet. If children need a little help getting started, prompt

them with a few examples. For instance, in this book, C is for confused. C could also be for *curious*, *caring*, and *calm*. F is for frustrated, and could also be for *fearful* and *funny*.

- Talk with children about the fact that there are so many different words for the ways we feel. Why do they think that is? What are some of their favorite feeling words, and why?

Share and Compare Feelings

F Is for Feelings gives adults a great way to share their own feelings and experiences in a way children can relate to. During or after reading the book together, share a time when you personally have felt one of the feelings in the book. Why did you feel that way? How did you deal with the feeling?

After reading, you may also want to talk about how you are feeling at the moment. For instance, you might say, "I am feeling quiet today." Try to be specific and use more than one feeling word. Work on communicating the degree of your emotion by saying things such as "I am a little bit upset," or "I am very excited!" Then share what you do to cope with your feelings. For example, you could say, "When I feel frustrated, it can help me if I remember to take deep breaths," or, "When I am very excited I feel like jumping up and down!"

Build Empathy

Empathy is the ability to feel compassion and understanding for others. The better equipped children are to recognize other people's feelings, the more likely they are to build strong, positive relationships at school, at home, and beyond. In school settings, children's ability to empathize has also been shown to reduce bullying.

To help children practice empathy, choose a feeling word from the book and ask children how they would respond to a friend who is experiencing this emotion. For example, if

you decide to talk about "A is for afraid," ask children what they would do if a friend or classmate were expressing or showing fear. What would they say? How could they help that person address the feeling?

Listen to Children's Feelings

The act of listening is a powerful way to communicate understanding and acknowledgment of the feelings a child may be experiencing. Being an open and attentive listener also helps show children that their feelings are normal and healthy.

Listening does not necessarily mean you need to solve the problem or "fix" the situation. It simply means hearing what a child is feeling. Adults and children both need time and space to experience their feelings. When caring adults listen, it gives children that space to naturally process their emotions.

Help Children Name and Say Their Feelings

Try listening for the feeling words a child expresses. When a child shares his or her feelings with you, talk a little and listen a *lot*. In addition, it can be helpful to openly and directly communicate what you have heard or understood about the child's feelings. This shows respect and supports emotional growth.

For example, name and verbalize as accurately as possible what you are hearing. Try to be straightforward and specific. For example, you might say, "I think that you are trying to show me that you are feeling really frustrated right now." Or you might ask, "Are you feeling worried about something? It seems like you're in an anxious mood. Is there any way I can help?"

It's okay to be unsure of what a child is expressing. You can offer suggestions, ask questions, and be tentative. The words in this book are a good starting point.

What to Do If You Are Concerned About a Child's Emotional Health

If a child is displaying or talking about extreme feelings, or is struggling significantly with making it through the day, it may be important to seek help from a qualified professional. Talking with a psychologist, social worker, or family physician can provide assistance in developing the best plan to help the child move toward emotional wellness.

Promote Acceptance

Always try to approach children with an attitude and message of acceptance toward their feelings.

Whatever role you play in a child's life, simply being open to what the child has to share and communicate can promote acceptance and support healthy emotional expression. For some children and adults, it can be difficult or uncomfortable to identify, talk about, and express emotions. But you can help children see that their feelings are natural and important. It is not healthy to stuff down or hide emotions. By learning how to express their feelings—especially the ones that may be uncomfortable—children can work through them in a positive way.

The ideas and feelings explored in *F Is for Feelings* help children understand that emotions—*all* emotions—are part of being human. We're all in this together!

About the Authors

Goldie Millar, Ph.D., is a clinical and school psychologist. She earned her Ph.D. in counseling psychology from the University of Toronto in 2003. Goldie has worked in hospital, forensic, community, and educational settings. She has a deep interest in children's mental health, emotional regulation, and evidence-based intervention strategies. Goldie lives in Ontario, Canada, with her husband and two young daughters. You can find her at www.fisforfeelings.com.

Lisa A. Berger, Ph.D., is a clinical, counseling, and rehabilitation psychologist who works with adolescents and adults in a private practice. In 2003, Lisa received her Ph.D. in psychology from the University of Toronto. She has practiced in hospitals, post-secondary institutions, and community-based settings. Lisa's professional interests include emotional health and wellness, psychological trauma, and emotion-based therapy. She lives in Ontario, Canada, with her husband and two daughters. You can find her at www.fisforfeelings.com.

About the Illustrator

Hazel Mitchell thinks the best feeling is when her illustrations make other people happy. She grew up and attended art college in England and has illustrated books for children, including *How to Talk to an Autistic Kid* and *One Word Pearl*. You can find out more about her work at www.hazelmitchell.com. Hazel lives in Maine.

Other Great Books from Free Spirit

I'm Like You, You're Like Me
A Book About Understanding and Appreciating Each Other
by Cindy Gainer, illustrated by Miki Sakamoto
48 pp., color, illust., HC & PB, 11¼" x 9¼".
Ages 3–8.

I Hate Everything!
A book about feeling angry
by Sue Graves,
illustrated by Desideria Guicciardini
28 pp., color, illust., HC, 7¾" x 9½".
Ages 4–8.

Zach Gets Frustrated
by William Mulcahy,
illustrated by Darren McKee
32 pp., color, illust., HC, 8" x 8".
Ages 5–8.

Feel Confident!
A book about self-esteem
by Cheri J. Meiners, M.Ed.,
illustrated by Elizabeth Allen
40 pp., color, illust., PB, 11¼" x 9¼".
Ages 4–8.

For pricing information, to place an order, or to request a free catalog, contact:
Free Spirit Publishing Inc. • 6325 Sandburg Road • Suite 100 • Minneapolis, MN 55427-3674
toll-free 800.735.7323 • local 612.338.2068 • fax 612.337.5050
help4kids@freespirit.com • freespirit.com